Contents

Assembly Tomorrow
for Key Stage 1

INTRODUCTION

Coming up with new and interesting ideas for assembly can often be an extremely difficult and time-consuming task. Ideally, of course, the subject matter of every assembly should have a clear moral message, should be motivating for pupils and be of a broadly Christian outlook. These guidelines were followed in the predecessor to this book, *Assembly Today*, and are also adhered to in this book where we include a new range of assembly ideas appropriate for all children regardless of their faith or cultural heritage.

The assemblies are arranged in school term order, although many can be used at other times in the school year as well. Each assembly has a moral or thought-provoking message (outlined under the 'AIM' heading), a visual or physically active element, a prayer and a suggested song or hymn.

For most of the assemblies you will need an overhead projector. In some instances, where the assembly is based on a story, we have provided silhouettes that need to be photocopied on to paper and then cut out (before the assembly) for display on the OHP. This creates a simple shadow puppet show that is certain to gain the children's full attention! For other story-based assemblies, a simple picture is provided that can be photocopied on to acetate and placed on the OHP to act as a visual aid while the story is being read out. The rest of the assemblies include stories with integrated pictures. These you can photocopy on to acetate and then place on the OHP so that children can listen to the story and follow the text with the accompanying picture cues. If you have plenty of preparation time, you could involve the children in the retelling of the story or they could even role-play the issues being addressed.

For some of the assembly ideas, you might simply want to follow the script (shown in italics) that is provided on the teacher's page, while for others you might decide to read the assembly notes first and then present it in your own words. Whichever style of presentation you choose, assemblies should be an enjoyable and thought-provoking experience for all concerned.

New beginnings

 AIM: To consider the season of autumn and the changes that take place across the four months of the autumn term.

PREPARATION

■ If you are planning to use an OHP, photocopy 'New beginnings' (page 4) on to an acetate sheet.

■ INTRODUCTION

Explain to the children that this is the start of a new school year. Lots of changes have taken place and most people are in a new class with a new teacher. We have had the summer holidays and this is the start of the term that we call the autumn term.

■ ASSEMBLY

Turn on the OHP but keep the acetate covered with a piece of paper.

Does anyone know what month it is now?

Hopefully the children will say that it is the month of September. (Move the paper down the screen to reveal *September*). Discuss the fact that September marks the end of the season called 'summer' and the beginning of the new season called 'autumn'.

What month comes after September?

Again somebody will volunteer the answer October. Discuss the fact that this is harvest time when all the fruit and vegetables are ripe and ready to be picked. October also marks changes in nature as the weather becomes very windy, animals begin hibernating and leaves turn brown and fall from the trees.

What month comes after October?

Many children will not know that November follows October. (Move the paper down and reveal *November*). Discuss the month of November when there will be lots of leaves on the ground and bonfire night takes place.

What month comes after November?

(Remove the paper altogether to show all four months.) Discuss the month of December and, if appropriate to your cultural setting, the fact that Christmas takes place in December. Can the children remember what December is like? You could remind them of the dark evenings, the cold weather, the bare trees, etc.

It would be worthwhile to remind the children of this assembly at the start of each of the following three months – learning the order of the months of the year is an objective for Year 1 pupils.

■ REFLECTION

Remind the children about the changes that will take place across the autumn term: the onset of darker nights, the colder weather, leaves falling off the trees, etc. You may also like to discuss some of the events that are happening in school.

Prayer

Dear Lord,
Thank you for the changing seasons. We thank you for the summer weather and the lovely long evenings that we have enjoyed. Help us to enjoy the autumn term. Help us to work hard at school, to make new friends and to welcome any new members to our school. Help us to enjoy being together, playing together and working together.

Amen

Song Harvest (Harlequin, 31: *A&C Black*)

New beginnings

September

October

November

December

The wise man and the foolish man

 AIM: To help children understand that to complete a task well it needs to be carefully thought out.

> **PREPARATION**
> ■ Photocopy 'The wise man and the foolish man' (page 6) and cut out the outlines ready to illustrate the story you are going to tell.

INTRODUCTION

At the beginning of the assembly ensure that pupils understand the meanings of the words *wise* and *foolish*. Can they think of simple examples of wise and foolish things? For example, it is wise to wear a coat when it rains but foolish to wear a coat when it is hot.

STORY

A wise man needed to build a new home. (Show wise man on OHP.)

He looked around until he found a very large flat rock. (Add this to picture.)

Slowly and carefully he built himself a house on the rock. (Place house on rock.)

A foolish man also needed to build a house. (Add foolish man to picture.)

He didn't want to waste time looking for just the right place so he decided to build his house on the sandy beach near to him. (Add sand to picture.)

He had very soon made himself a new and comfortable home. (Add home on sand.)

One winter's day there was a terrible storm. It poured with rain and the wind blew. The house on the solid rock stood firmly in its place and the wise man was safe inside. The house on the sand, however, began to collapse as the wind, rain and waves washed away the sand beneath it. (Remove house from sand and replace it with ruined house.)

The foolish man was very unhappy as his house fell down before his eyes.

REFLECTION

Ask pupils why the house on the sand fell down. Introduce the word *foundations*. Explain that this story is a parable from the Bible and that a parable is a story with a message/lesson. Ask pupils what they think the lesson of the story is. Accept their ideas and ensure that they understand that anything we do in life needs to have strong foundations. What are the foundations of a house and what do they do? Have the children heard of Foundation Stage at school? Why is it called Foundation Stage? Can the children understand that strong houses need to be built on good foundations in the same way that successful learning higher up the school needs solid foundation work in the early years?

Prayer

Dear Lord,
Help us to prepare for the tasks we tackle each day so that we always get the best results that we can. Help us to do our best and to be pleased with the work we do.

Amen

Song The Building Song (Alleluya, 59: *A&C Black*)

The wise man and the foolish man

Building new homes

AIM: To help children learn that when people work as a team they achieve the best results.

PREPARATION

■ Photocopy 'Building new homes' (page 8) and cut out the shapes of the house, the scaffolding and the people to show on the OHP.

■ INTRODUCTION

Remind pupils of the story about the wise man and the foolish man (page 5). Both men built houses but one was more successful than the other. Can they remember the reason why this was?

Does anyone remember the word 'foundations'?

Remind the children of the various ways in which the word foundations is used: foundations of a house, Foundation Stage at school and why it is called that. Remind them that strong houses need to be built on good foundations in the same way that successful learning higher up the school needs solid foundation work in the early years.

Ask the children how many of them have seen new homes being built. This can be particularly appropriate if there is a building site near the school.

■ ASSEMBLY

Place the picture of the modern house in the centre of the OHP screen. Add the scaffolding and ask the children to explain why it is there. Ask them to tell you what sort of people are involved in the building of a new home, e.g. architect, planners, brick-layers, carpenters, electricians, plumbers, roofers, decorators, plasterers, etc. As each is mentioned add the appropriate shape around the edge of the house picture. You may decide to ask the child who suggests the job to come up and place the shape on the picture. Discuss what each tradesperson does.

■ REFLECTION

Help pupils to understand how these different professions have to work together to build a house successfully and how they have to cooperate throughout the process. Ask pupils to suggest tasks where they have had to work with others in a cooperative manner, e.g. team games, group work, etc.

Prayer

Dear Lord,
Just like builders who work as a team to build new houses, please help us to work well together each day at school and at home whether working or playing.

Amen

♫
Song   The Building Song (Alleluya, 59: *A&C Black*)

Building new homes

Days of the week

 AIM: To think about doing good things every day.

PREPARATION

■ Photocopy 'Days of the week' (page 10) on to an acetate sheet, then cut the sheet into separate pieces for each day, keeping the rhyme as a separate piece.

▨ INTRODUCTION

Ask the pupils what day it is today, then place the appropriate 'day' on the OHP. You could use the opportunity to discuss the other days of the week by asking what day it was yesterday, what day it will be tomorrow etc, placing the acetates on the screen as the pupils answer. Most of the days are phonically regular and you could help the children to read the words by covering them and revealing one syllable at a time. Once this is completed, remove all the acetates except today's.

▨ ASSEMBLY

Put the days of the week rhyme on the OHP. You could use this rhyme to reinforce the pupils' knowledge of the order of the days of the week. Learning this order is an objective for Year 1 pupils.

> *Monday's child is good at school.*
>
> *Tuesday's child never breaks the rules.*
>
> *Wednesday's child works hard all day.*
>
> *Thursday's child just likes to play.*
>
> *Friday's child tries hard to win.*
>
> *Saturday's child goes for a swim.*
>
> *Sunday's child takes care of friends,*
>
> *Such good friendship never ends.*

Ask the children 'which day of the week' child is most like them or are they like all of the children? As an extension activity to do later, you could ask some of the older pupils to make up their own days of the week rhyme.

Discuss what is going to happen today, including any special events but also highlighting the more routine things. Ask the children to think of any things that are going to happen today – ask them to think especially about good things that are going to happen. What are they looking forward to? Now ask them to think about what they might do today as individuals, e.g.

> *How are you going to be kind to someone today?*
>
> *How are you going to help someone today?*
>
> *Who is going to help you today and what will they do to help you?*

▨ REFLECTION

Encourage the children to value today and every day and to think about how each of us can help each other and be kind to each other.

Prayer

> *Dear Lord,*
> *Please help us to be kind to each other today and every day. We thank you for giving us this day – help us to make the most of it.*
>
> > *Amen*

Song

Father, we thank you for the night (Someone's Singing Lord, 1: *A&C Black*)
or
Each day is different (Harlequin, 43: *A&C Black*)

Days of the week

Monday

Tuesday

Wednesday

Thursday

Friday

Saturday

Sunday

Monday's child is good at school.
Tuesday's child never breaks the rules.
Wednesday's child works hard all day.
Thursday's child just likes to play.
Friday's child tries hard to win.
Saturday's child goes for a swim.
Sunday's child takes care of friends,
Such good friendship never ends.

Potatoes

AIM: To encourage children to appreciate the uniqueness of all living things.

PREPARATION

■ Have a variety of potatoes available.

■ Photocopy 'Potatoes' (page 12) on to acetate for use with an OHP.

▨ INTRODUCTION

Pupils should be asked to put up their hands if they eat potatoes. Explain that as this is harvest time, it is a good time to think about all the vegetables that we eat but in this instance we are going to focus on potatoes. Potatoes that were planted in the spring are now ready to be harvested – they grow in groups in the soil and they have to be dug out of the ground. Next the children can be asked how many ways potatoes can be prepared and eaten, e.g. baked, roasted, mashed, chipped, made into crisps, put in pies, put in stews, cottage pie, etc. Accept their contributions and encourage them to appreciate the many different uses that potatoes have.

▨ ASSEMBLY

Show them either the potatoes you have brought to the assembly or the 'Potatoes' acetate. Point out that each potato is unique and that even if you had brought in a thousand potatoes, no two of them would be identical. Look at the differences between the ones they are looking at, either the ones you have brought in or those shown on the screen.

Lead on to the fact that things made in factories are usually the same but in the natural world, everything is different which makes each living thing very special. You may need to use and explain the word *unique*. Finally read with the children, the potato poem on the acetate. Remind them that although potatoes are good for us, we should not eat too many of them because too much of any food may not be good for our health.

▨ REFLECTION

If appropriate to your setting, you may decide to talk about how special and different each creature, plant and vegetable created by God is, and how much he cares. 'If he cares enough to make each potato different just imagine how much he must care about each person he makes.'

Prayer

Dear Lord,
We give you thanks for the vegetables in the harvest and the care with which you created them all. We thank you too for all the people that care for the plants as they grow, all the gardeners and farmers that tend them each day. Help us to remember how much you care for every single one of us every day.

Amen

Song   Paint-box (Harlequin, 32: *A&C Black*)

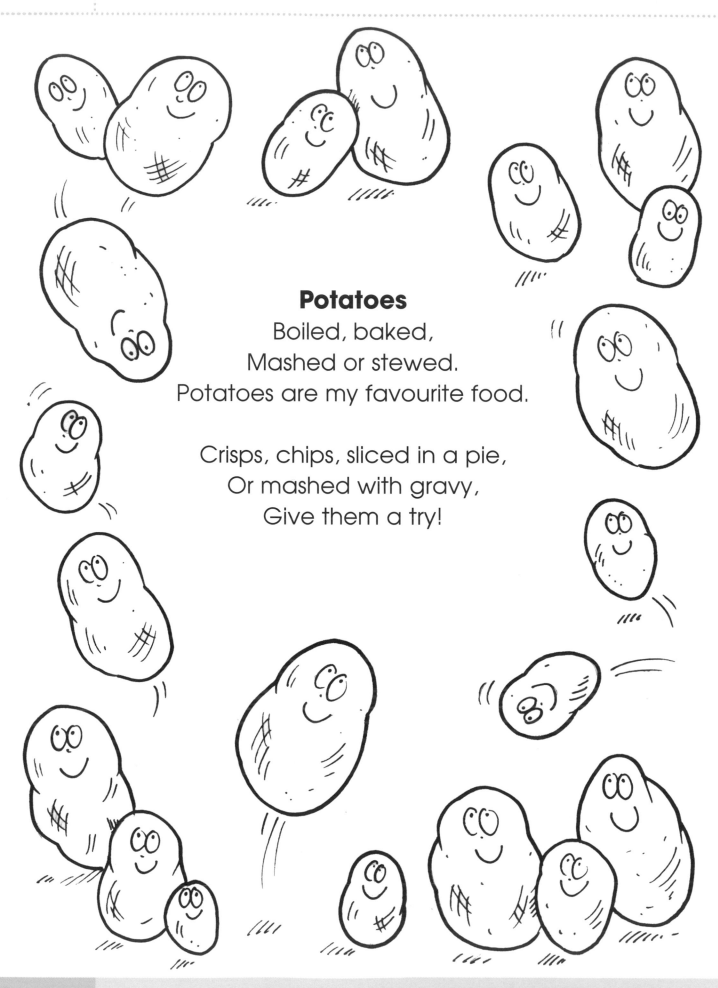

Potatoes
Boiled, baked,
Mashed or stewed.
Potatoes are my favourite food.

Crisps, chips, sliced in a pie,
Or mashed with gravy,
Give them a try!

Goldilocks and the three bears

 AIM: To consider right and wrong in the context of the well-known fairy tale Goldilocks.

PREPARATION

- Photocopy and cut out the silhouettes from 'Goldilocks and the three bears' (pages 15 -16).
- You may like to spread the story over two assemblies by stopping the first one after the porridge or the chairs!

INTRODUCTION

Ask the children if they know the story of Goldilocks. Explain that it is a very old story and there are many different versions of it. Today's story is one version.

STORY

One day Goldilocks went for a walk in the woods all by herself.

Was that a sensible thing to do? (Accept pupils' answers and stress the dangers of going anywhere alone.)

There she is. (Place the silhouette of Goldilocks on the screen.)

Goldilocks walked along happily for a while and then she felt very hungry.

"I'd love something to eat," she said to herself. Just then she saw a little cottage. "I'll go in here and see if I can find anything," she said.
Was that a sensible thing to do? (Accept pupils' answers and stress the dangers of going into a strange house. Place the silhouette of the table and the bowls of porridge on the screen.)

When Goldilocks went inside the cottage she saw a table with three bowls of porridge sitting on it.
"I am hungry," she said to herself. "Nobody would mind if I had a little bit to eat." And, because she was quite a greedy girl, she dipped a spoon in the biggest bowl of porridge and tried it. "Oh, I don't like that one," she said. "So I will try this one." She tried the middle-sized bowl of porridge. "Oh, I don't like that one," she said. "So I will try this one." She tried the smallest bowl of porridge. "Um, this one is yummy," she said and she ate it all up.

Was that a sensible thing to do? (Accept pupils' answers, encouraging them to understand why Goldilocks should not be eating somebody else's food.)

(Remove the table and place the silhouettes of the three chairs on the screen, ensuring that the small chair has a separate leg in position but that the children cannot see that it is separate. At appropriate points in the story position the 'sitting Goldilocks' on each chair until the final chair breaks.)

After she had eaten the porridge Goldilocks felt quite tired. "I need to sit down," she said to herself. She tried sitting on a great big hard chair. "Oh, I don't like that one," she said. "So I will try this one." She tried sitting on a quite big soft chair but she just sank down into it. "Oh, I don't like that one," she said. "So I will try this one." She tried sitting on a smaller chair. "I like this one," she said and she squeezed herself down into it. Unfortunately, she was a bit too big for this chair and it suddenly gave a loud crack and one of the legs fell off. "Oh dear," said Goldilocks. "People really should make better chairs. I could have hurt myself."

Was that a sensible thing to say? (Accept pupils' answers, encouraging them to understand that Goldilocks should not have broken somebody else's property.)

By now, Goldilocks was really tired. "I wonder what's up here," she said to herself and began climbing the stairs.

Goldilocks and the three bears

Was that a sensible thing to do? (Accept pupils' answers while removing the chairs from the screen and replacing them with the beds.)

Goldilocks tried lying on the biggest bed. "Oh, I don't like that one," she said. "So I will try this one." She tried the middle-sized bed. "Oh, I don't like that one," she said. "So I will try this one." And she tried the smallest bed. "This is very comfy," she said and then she yawned loudly and fell fast asleep.

Not long after that the three bears, who owned the house, came home. They had not been out for very long so they were surprised to find that Little Bear's porridge had been eaten and that his chair had been broken. "Somebody's been in our house," they said. They were a bit frightened so they held on to each other as they went up the stairs. When they saw Goldilocks they had such a shock that they all yelled "Ahhh!"

At this noise, Goldilocks woke up. She was so frightened that she yelled "Ahhh!" too.

Luckily, as the three bears were very nice bears they forgave Goldilocks and took her straight back home to her mum and dad.

▦ REFLECTION

What do you think Goldilocks' mum said to her when she got home?

Discuss the various issues that the story raises, including: safety, taking other people's things, causing damage to other people's property. Stress that Goldilocks didn't mean to be naughty and that the story had a happy ending!

Prayer

Dear Lord,
Help to keep us safe. Help us to remember not to go out on our own. Help us to avoid taking or damaging other people's property.

Amen

Song

(To provide a contrast to the story)
Stand up, clap hands, shout "Thank you, Lord" (Someone's Singing Lord, 14: *A&C Black*)

Goldilocks and the three bears

Goldilocks and the three bears

Every hour of every day

 AIM: To think about doing good things throughout the day.

PREPARATION

■ Photocopy 'Every hour of every day' (page 18) on to an acetate sheet, then cut out the clock face and the two separate hands.

■ **INTRODUCTION**

Ask the pupils what time it is now. (Place the acetate clock face and the two separate clock hands in the appropriate places.)

■ **ASSEMBLY**

I'm going to show you a different time on the clock.

Can you tell me the time the clock shows now? (Change the hands to show 7 o'clock.) *This is the time when I get up in the morning.*

Can you tell me the time the clock shows now? (Change the hands to show 9 o'clock.) *That's about the time that school starts.*

Continue the process, showing times throughout the school day and into the evening up to bedtime.

Ask the pupils again what time it is now. (Place the acetate clock face and the two separate clock hands in the appropriate places.)

The time has moved on since we started assembly – it was … and it's now …

The Primary Framework for literacy and mathematics suggests that most Year 1 children will learn to read the time to the hour and half hour and that most Year 2 children will be able to read the time to the quarter hour. This assembly provides the opportunity for children to reflect on what happens throughout the day and their role in the things that happen while, at the same time, providing practice in the mathematical skills of both reading the time and of understanding time intervals.

■ **REFLECTION**

Ask the pupils to think about the whole day, encouraging them to think about doing kind and helpful things all through the day.

Prayer

Dear Lord,
Please help us to be helpful and kind to other people all day long. Help us to try hard not to argue with other people and not to hurt other people by being unkind to them in any way. Help us all to have a good day. Not everything will be easy today but help us to try hard to deal with everything in a cheerful way

Amen

Song

Thank you Lord (Come and Praise, 32: *BBC*)

Every hour of every day

Body language

 AIM: To help pupils realise that facial expressions and body language are an important part of life.

PREPARATION

■ Photocopy 'Getting dressed' (page 20) on to an acetate sheet and have the cut outs ready for the OHP presentation (you may not need all of them).

■ **INTRODUCTION**

Tell pupils that today they will be thinking about how they get dressed and prepare themselves for the day ahead. (Put the blank child shape on the OHP with the plain head shape; underwear is already on the figure.)

■ **ASSEMBLY**

Ask pupils how they get dressed in the morning and in what order they do things. As you accept each answer, discuss it briefly and if appropriate add the item to the picture, e.g. if cleaning teeth is mentioned, talk about the importance of keeping teeth clean and healthy but explain that you do not have a toothbrush to add to the picture.

Once the figure is fully clothed, explain that we would all like to look as smart as we can and that our clothes are an important part of who we are but that one of the most important features is missing from the picture – the face! Show them the faces that can be added to the outline and ask which they think would be the best one to add, and why. Hopefully they will choose the happy face.

Finally ask a child (preferably one dressed in a similar way to the OHP picture) to be your helper. The helper should be in a position where everyone can see him/her. Instruct the child to make him/herself look as grumpy as possible, as if he/she is really cross about something. Point out to everyone that not only does their face change but so does the way they stand. You may want to tell them that this is called 'body language'. Now ask the helper to look as cheerful as possible, as though they have just found out they are going to a party. Again point out the changes in stance as well as facial expression. Thank your helper and invite him/her to sit down again.

■ **REFLECTION**

Ask pupils to think for a moment about how different it feels to smile than to frown and how smiling can actually make you feel better. Ask them to think about the implications of body language in sowing others that you are feeling friendly towards them.

Prayer

Dear Lord,
Help us to show others our good mood throughout the day. Help us to be smiling people with a welcoming look and with actions and words to match our smiles. Father, we thank you for giving us faces, bodies, hands, feet and voices that we can use to show our happiness and love towards others.

Amen

Song

Magic penny (Alleluya, 10: *A&C Black*)
or
Father I thank you (Everyone's singing Lord, 4: *A&C Black*)

Body language

Preparing for Christmas

 AIM: To encourage the personal qualities valued by all major faiths.

PREPARATION

- Photocopy 'Preparing for Christmas' (page 22) on to an acetate sheet ready to show on the OHP.
- Have available some coloured markers to write in the baubles.
- You may decide to let a child colour the tree shape green and the star yellow prior to the assembly.

▨ INTRODUCTION

Show pupils the picture on the OHP and tell them that they are going to help you to think about how to decorate the baubles on it. They may need an explanation of the word 'bauble'. At this point pupils may be keen to tell you about the ways in which they decorate trees at home.

▨ ASSEMBLY

Our way of decorating the tree today will be different from any trees you might be decorating at home. We are going to think about the qualities we want to take into Christmas with us. This means that we want to think of words that describe the sort of people we are or that we would like to be.

Start the ideas off by suggesting that being kind is important at Christmas and of course during the rest of the year too. Write the word 'kind' in large letters on one of the baubles. Ask pupils for other ideas, e.g. happy, friendly, helpful, thankful, smiling, sharing, caring, giving, etc. Accept all contributions and write the most appropriate ones on the baubles.

▨ REFLECTION

Encourage pupils to think about their personal qualities and how they should use these qualities in a positive way, not only at Christmas but also throughout the year. Help them to understand that the way they live their lives and behave towards others is much more important than presents, parties, etc. An effective way to follow this assembly up in the classroom is to have a Christmas tree wall display on which each child can add a bauble shape containing their name and a positive quality they have.

Prayer

Dear Lord,
Help us to help others to enjoy the Christmas season by being kind and caring towards others. We thank you Lord for all that you do for us at this happy time of the year and hope that we may live our lives in the way you would like us to.

Amen

Song

Jesus hands were kind hands (Someone's Singing Lord, 33: *A&C Black*)
O Christmas Tree, O Christmas Tree (Carol, Gaily Carol, 41: *A&C Black*)

Preparing for Christmas

Springtime

 AIM: To consider the seasons of winter and spring and the changes that take place across the four months of the spring term.

PREPARATION

■ Photocopy 'Springtime' (page 24) on to an acetate sheet for display on the OHP.

▨ INTRODUCTION

Explain to the children that this is the start of the new year. *We have just had the Christmas holidays and this is the start of the term that we call the 'spring term'.* Discuss the fact that it is still winter now but that the spring comes at the end of the term.

▨ ASSEMBLY

Turn on the OHP but keep the acetate covered with a piece of paper.

Does anyone know what month it is now?

Hopefully the children will say that it is the month of January. (Move the paper down the screen to reveal *January*.) Discuss the fact that January is a winter month with cold weather and darker evenings.

What month comes after January?

Discuss February, the shortest month of the year, which is still very cold but signs of spring, such as snowdrops, begin to appear.

What month comes after February?

(Move the paper down to reveal *March*). Discuss March – often very cold at the start but with more flowers beginning to appear and the green buds of leaves showing on trees.

What month comes after March?

(Remove the paper altogether to show all four months.) Discuss that in the month of April leaves begin to appear on trees, birds such as swallows and house martins return to England from the hot countries in Africa, the evenings are no longer dark and the weather begins to feel a lot warmer.

It would be worthwhile to remind the children of this assembly at the start of each of the following three months – learning the order of the months of the year is an objective for Year 1 pupils.

▨ REFLECTION

Remind the children about the changes that will take place across the spring term – the dark nights and cold weather that we have at the start of the term, then the warmer weather, the lighter evenings, the flowers and leaves coming out and the return of the swallows at the end of the term.

Prayer

Dear Lord,
Thank you for the changing seasons. We thank you for the cold weather of the winter and the warmer weather that will come in the spring. Help us to enjoy the spring term. Help us to work hard at school and to make new friends. Help us to enjoy being together, playing together and working together.

Amen

Song

January (Harlequin, 2: *A&C Black*)

Springtime

January

February

March

April

Twinkle, twinkle little star

 AIM: To consider the awe and wonder of space and the stars.

PREPARATION

- Choose a dark day to present this assembly or choose a room where you can shut out the light.
- Photocopy 'Twinkle, twinkle little star' (page 26) on to an acetate sheet and place this on the OHP.
- Find a piece of paper big enough to completely cover the plate of the OHP then cut out a very small star-shaped hole. Place this sheet over the poem so that it can't be read.

INTRODUCTION

Once the children are settled turn out all the lights in the hall and turn on the OHP. Ask the children what they can see.

ASSEMBLY

Discuss the picture of the star. Ask the children when they might see stars – obviously at night but point out that we can only see them when it's not cloudy. Have they looked at stars? Have they noticed how many there are in the sky? Do they know that stars are thousands of miles away in space and that nobody has ever visited them? Do they know that lots of them are bigger than the sun but they look so tiny because they are so far away?

The next time there's a clear night, you could ask your mum or dad or the adult who is caring for you to take you outside to look at the stars in the sky. If you look carefully you might see a tiny light that is moving – this won't be a star but it could be an aeroplane very high in the sky. If you are really lucky, you might see what is called a 'shooting star'. It's not really a star at all but a meteorite, which is a lump of rock that is often mistaken for a star.

Remove the paper with the star-shaped hole from the screen to reveal the poem and read this with the children. Many of them will probably be familiar with the poem as a song.

REFLECTION

There are so many stars in the sky that twinkle when it's dark at night that it would be impossible to count them all. You may like to ask the children if they know what the word 'heaven' means and where it is.

Sometimes we call the sky above us, when it's full of stars, 'the heavens' and we call the sun, the moon, the planets and the stars 'heavenly bodies'. Perhaps it's because when we look up at the millions of stars in the sky it seems like heaven.

Prayer

Dear Lord,
We thank you for all the stars that twinkle in the night sky. We thank you for the sun, the moon and for the earth where we live. Help to look after our special earth.

Amen

Song Can you count the stars? (Someone's Singing Lord, 25: *A&C Black*)

Twinkle, twinkle little star

Twinkle, twinkle, little star,
How I wonder what you are!
Up above the world so high,
Like a diamond in the sky!
Twinkle, twinkle, little star,
How I wonder what you are!

Look into my eyes

 AIM: To appreciate our eyes and all that we can see.

> **PREPARATION**
> ■ Photocopy 'Look into my eyes' (page 28) on to an acetate sheet. Place it on the OHP
> with a piece of paper over the poem so that you can reveal it later.

■ INTRODUCTION

Ask the pupils to look at the person next to them.

What colour eyes does the person next to you have?

Discuss the different eye colours, giving suggestions of the colours they may see: blue, green, grey, light brown, dark brown.

■ ASSEMBLY

Turn on the OHP and reveal the drawing of an eye.

Look at this picture of an eye. Does it look like the eyes of the person next to you? What's different about it?

Hopefully the children will point out that it doesn't show colour and of course, that there is only one eye shown.

The picture doesn't show the eye colour does it? Let's look at the parts of the eye. Can you see the eyelashes? The eyelashes help to keep things out of our eyes. Look at this part – we call it the white part of the eye. The part in the middle is the very dark part. That's the part that we actually see through and it has a special name – it's called 'the pupil'. Have a look at your neighbour again – can you see the pupil in each eye? The bit around the pupil is the coloured part of the eye and that's called 'the iris'.

Why do you think that we have two eyes?

Accept answers and then explain 'if necessary' it's because we can judge distance better with two eyes. You could demonstrate this by asking a child to come out to the front of the hall for an experiment. Making sure that all the children can see the demonstration, ask the child to touch an object that is clearly in front of her/him but for which s/he has to reach forward. You could ask the child to touch the end of your finger, for example, then ask her/him to close one eye tightly and to touch the object again. Using only one eye it's likely that the child will miss.

■ REFLECTION

Encourage pupils to consider the variety of eyes and how every person is different. Encourage them to be thankful for their eyes and the things they can see. You could raise the subject of blind people and how life can be very difficult for them but how they find ways to deal with every day living. Some blind people are assisted by 'seeing dogs' (guide dogs). Show the children the poem and read it through with them, perhaps encouraging them to add actions to the words.

Prayer

Dear Lord,
Thank you for our eyes and all the things we can see around us. Thank you for making all of us different and for making every one of us very special.

Amen

Song

He gave me eyes so I could see (Someone's Singing Lord, 19: *A&C Black*)

Look into my eyes

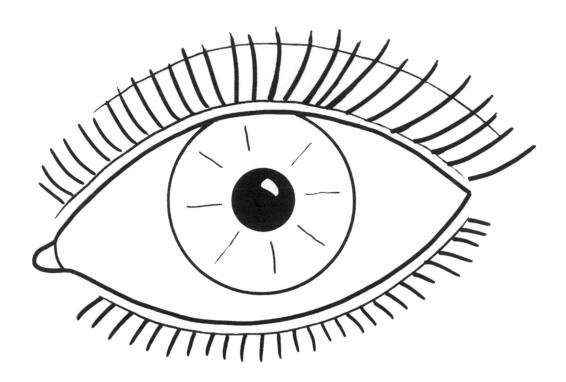

With our eyes
We can see.
You and me,
We can see.
We can wink,
We can blink.
Eyes are special,
Don't you think?

Fingers and thumbs

AIM: To help children to appreciate their bodies but particularly their hands, fingers and thumbs.

PREPARATION

■ Photocopy 'Fingers and thumbs' (page 30) on to paper or card then cut out the silhouettes of the hand with the thumb up and the hand with the finger pointed.

■ INTRODUCTION

Ask the pupils what it means when someone gives you the 'thumbs up'. You may like to demonstrate or to show the silhouette. Accept answers and encourage the children to accept that 'thumbs up' means something good. Now discuss 'thumbs down' and turn the silhouette upside down (meaning something is not good).

■ ASSEMBLY

We've talked about thumbs – let's have a look at the other fingers.

Place the silhouette of the pointing finger on the screen.

Can you see which finger is being used now? What's it doing? It's pointing isn't it? That's a very important finger – it's called 'the first finger' or 'the index finger'. We can use it for pointing; we can use it for telling someone off by wagging it. It's often used with the thumb. Look, we can pick things up with it and the thumb working together. If we use both hands we can use our thumbs and first fingers to do up buttons. Let's look at the next finger. I need to have some help with this.

Invite a volunteer to come out and place her/his hand on the glass screen of the OHP, but do check that the screen is not too hot. Briefly look again at the thumb and the first finger, then introduce the second finger.

This finger is called 'the second finger' or 'the middle finger'. The next finger is called 'the third finger', or we sometimes call it 'the ring finger' because people often have a ring on this one. And the last finger is 'the fourth finger' or 'the little finger'. If we count the thumb, how many fingers do we have altogether on one hand? And how many do we have on both hands?

You may like to ask your volunteer to place both hands on the screen so that the younger children can count all ten fingers.

■ REFLECTION

Encourage the children to realise that all the fingers are important and that they work together well.

Prayer

*Dear Lord,
Thank you for our hands and our fingers and thumbs. Thank you for the way our fingers and thumbs work together to do so many things for us.*

Amen

Song   Hands to work and feet to run (Someone's Singing Lord, 21: *A&C Black*)

Fingers and thumbs

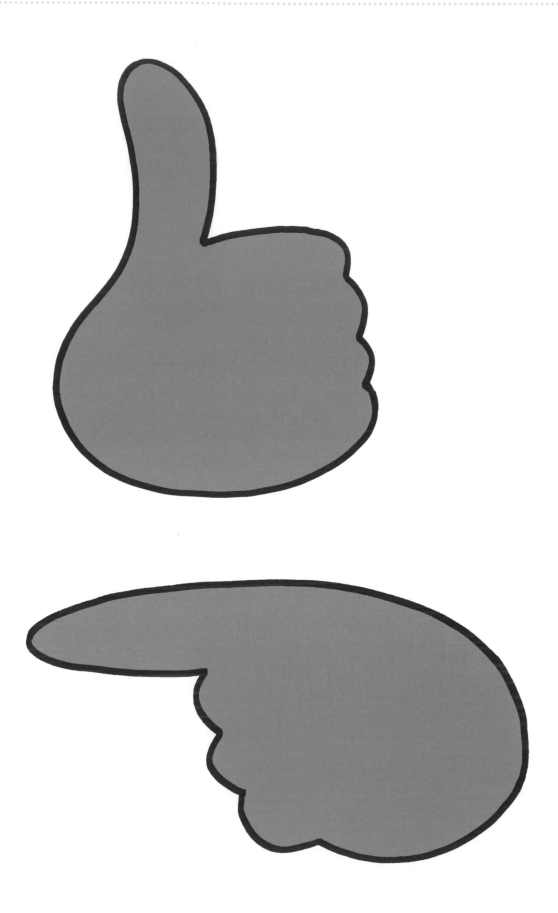

It's raining!

 AIM: To consider the importance of water.

PREPARATION

- This assembly is ideal for a rainy day.
- Photocopy 'It's raining!' (page 32) and cut out the silhouettes of raindrops. You may need to make two copies to provide lots of drops.

INTRODUCTION

Suggest that the children look out of the window.

What is the weather like today?

ASSEMBLY

Turn on the OHP and place a raindrop silhouette on the screen.

It always seems such a nuisance when it rains doesn't it? Can you tell me any bad things about rain?

Pupils may make suggestions such as: you can't play outside, washing won't dry, you get wet if you have to go out, you have to wear a coat, etc. Accept contributions and for each one add a raindrop to the screen.

Too much rain can be very bad because it can cause floods.

Discuss any floods that have been in the news recently and explain how difficult it can be for people when floods block the roads, damage bridges or spread into houses ruining carpets and furniture. If appropriate, and depending on the sensitivity of the children in your audience, discuss the floods that are so severe they cause loss of life. Ask the children if they know the story about a flood that appears in the Bible and praise any children who can remember the story of Noah and his ark.

Now can you tell me any good things about rain?

The children may find it harder to think of good things and you may have to prompt them with ideas such as: it helps the plants to grow, it fills ponds for wildlife to live in, it provides the water for us to drink. Accept contributions and for each one add a raindrop to the screen.

What would happen if we didn't have rain?

Again, accept responses and for each one add a raindrop to the screen. Accept ideas such as, the land would be dry, nothing could grow, people would starve and maybe die, fishes wouldn't have homes, we couldn't drink or wash, etc.

REFLECTION

Point out that we are very lucky in this country because it rains regularly and this provides enough water for us to drink and to help all our plants and crops to grow. Encourage the children to think about other countries where sometimes there is no rain for a very long time. Contrast this with the flooding problems caused by sudden or prolonged rainfall.

Prayer

Dear Lord,
Thank you for the rain that you bring us, to give us water to drink, water to wash in and water to help the plants to grow.

Amen

Song   Water of Life (Come and Praise, 11: *BBC*)

It's raining!

Superheroes

AIM: To help children to think about the personal qualities of those people they most like to be with.

PREPARATION

■ Either have the 'Superheroes' OHP (page 34) ready for presentation and some OHP marker pens, or have some badge-sized circle stickers ready to write on and to stick on to children.

▨ INTRODUCTION

Children should be asked about superheroes that they may have heard of, e.g. Superman, Wonderwoman, Spiderman, etc. Talk about their special powers and encourage pupils to also think about their personal qualities, e.g. kindness, caring, etc. Introduce the idea that these heroes/heroines would not be admired if they were unkind people. You may wish to remind pupils that these are fictional characters and that real people don't have superhuman powers such as X-ray vision!

▨ ASSEMBLY

Talk about the fact that none of the children in the assembly have superhero powers but that they all can be 'super children' by using their personal qualities for the good of others. At this point, either invite a child to join you at the front (girl or boy or one of each), or show the OHP sheet (page 34).

Ask what makes an ideal 'super child'. Can the children think of simple words or phrases that could describe suitable attributes of the super child's character? Hopefully you will receive answers such as 'kindness', 'good manners', 'being helpful', 'hard-working'. Don't accept answers that are not personality characteristics, e.g. 'can run fast' is not appropriate. Accept all appropriate contributions and either write the attribute on a sticker for the child to wear or write it in one of the circles on the OHP.

Ask pupils to think about how many of the good qualities they have thought of today they show every day in their school and home lives. If appropriate to your school setting, you may wish to talk about the kindness and help shown by Jesus, but you should take great care to ensure pupils do not confuse religious characters with fictional superheroes.

▨ REFLECTION

Most of us can never do what some of the superheroes in stories can do, but we can all be 'super people', by living our lives in a way that makes the most of all our skills and talents both for ourselves and for helping other people too. We can be kind, helpful and friendly. We can be cheerful and smiling. We can be polite and hardworking. You could also add other attributes that have been mentioned by other children.

Prayer

Dear Lord,

Help us to be super children each day, to think of the needs of others before ourselves and to try our hardest in all that we do. Help us to be kind, helpful, friendly, cheerful and smiling. Help us to be polite and hardworking.

Amen

Song

Magic Penny (Alleluya, 10: *A&C Black*)
Jesus hands were kind hands (Someone's Singing Lord, 33: *A&C Black*)

Superheroes

Safety signs

AIM: To help children understand the need for rules to ensure their safety, and to encourage them to care about their own safety and that of others.

PREPARATION

■ Photocopy 'Safety signs' (page 36) on to acetate and have it ready on the OHP, covered with pieces of paper, so that when it is switched on you can reveal one picture at a time.

▨ INTRODUCTION

Ask the children to look around the room to see if they can spot any signs. If there aren't any, ask them to think about signs they see around the school, e.g. a sign for the secretary's office, a sign on a door, etc.

▨ ASSEMBLY

Switch on the OHP and show the signs one at a time. For each one, ask the pupils what the sign says and, if appropriate, whom the sign is for and where it might be found. Now ask pupils what all the signs have in common. Pupils should realise that these signs are all designed to keep people safe. The signs are a way of showing rules. There are rules that are designed to keep people safe and the signs are a reminder of the rules.

Let's look at the signs again. What rule does the sign remind us of? (Reveal the lollipop sign and prompt children to appreciate that it tells car drivers to slow down because children are crossing the road.)

What rule does this sign tell us about? (Show the 'Danger No Entry' sign and explain that it warns us not to go near something because it's dangerous.)

Discuss each of the signs in turn and for each one decide what rule the sign is telling us about i.e. a warning that we shouldn't go into the water because it is too deep, a rule that we shouldn't touch the electric cables because we will get an electric shock, a rule that we should wear a seat belt so that we are safer in the car or on an aeroplane. Ask pupils to tell you about the rules in school that are there for their own safety and for the well-being of all pupils.

▨ REFLECTION

Encourage pupils to think quietly about the rules that they follow each day and how important it is to follow them in order to stay safe and happy.

We don't have many signs in school that tell us about the school rules. We don't always needs signs because we know the rules. For example, we don't have a sign saying 'don't run in the corridors' but we know that we shouldn't because it's not safe.

You may also like to discuss with the children other rules that are particularly relevant to your school.

Prayer

Dear Lord,
We thank you for keeping us safe each day. Help us to always obey the rules that are there to help us lead safe and happy lives. Help us to think about other people and to always make sure that we help them to be safe and happy.

Amen

Song   We're Going Home (Someone's Singing Lord. 59: *A&C Black*)

Safety signs

Rescuers

AIM: To help children appreciate the bravery of people who do potentially dangerous jobs for the good of others.

PREPARATION

- Photocopy 'Rescuers' (page 38) on to acetate and cut out the pictures for presentation.

▨ INTRODUCTION

Ask pupils what it might mean when they hear a siren from a vehicle in the street. Accept their answers, which hopefully will include the emergency services.

▨ ASSEMBLY

As these questions are answered, put up the appropriate acetate picture and discuss the possible dangers that might be faced by these people as they do their jobs. Ask pupils who would be called when people need rescuing at sea. Put up the picture of the lifeboat. Explain that lifeboat crews often have to go out to sea in terrible storms to rescue people whose boats have been damaged by the strong winds and rough waves. If the lifeboat didn't come to their rescue, then these people could drown.

Can pupils think of any other people they might need when they are in a dangerous situation? The responses from this will give you a chance to discuss the fact that the armed forces also may be involved in dangerous situations. Point out that the work of the armed forces, as seen on news broadcasts, usually takes place in other countries (pictures of forces personnel are included on the sheet).

You may also be offered ideas about specialist rescuers, depending on the area in which you live, e.g. mountain 'search and rescue' teams.

▨ REFLECTION

Encourage pupils to think about the bravery of the people who may regularly be putting the safety of others above their own. Remind children of the brave people who have been discussed.

Prayer

Dear Lord,
We ask you to give strength and courage to the people who help to keep us safe each day and those who are ready to rescue us from dangerous situations. We thank you for all these brave people.

Amen

Song   Magic penny (Alleluya, 10: *A&C Black*)

Rescuers

Andrew Brodie: Assembly Tomorrow KS1 © A&C Black Publishers Ltd. 2008

Thank you

AIM: To help pupils appreciate the importance of acknowledging all the good things in their lives.

PREPARATION

■ Photocopy 'Thank you' (page 40) on to an acetate sheet ready for display on the OHP.

■ Have ready coloured markers to add words to the picture.

▨ INTRODUCTION

Show pupils the OHP picture and ask them to read the words in the speech bubble.

▨ ASSEMBLY

Ask the children if they know other ways of saying thank you, e.g.

• in another language (particularly appropriate if English isn't the first language)
• the way in which a baby first learns the word (Ta)
• or shortening the term – thanks

Add one of these terms to the empty speech bubble. Other appropriate words may be scattered around the picture. Next ask the pupils to think about and then suggest situations in which they might use the words 'thank you'. They may come up with examples such as:

• thanking someone for a birthday present
• thanking someone for opening a door
• thanking someone for passing something
• thanking someone for cooking a meal
• thanking someone for a lift
• thanking someone for a party

Reinforce the idea that each time they use 'thank you' it usually means something good has happened or something has been given to them.

▨ REFLECTION

Ask pupils to think about how it makes them feel when someone says 'thank you' to them and how they perhaps feel a little disappointed when someone seems not to care enough to say it. Use simple examples for this, such as when one child passes another a pencil, or when giving out a party invitation. Through these examples, help pupils to understand how important these simple words are. If appropriate to your situation, you may then point out the importance of remembering to say 'thank you' to God for the whole world that he has given us. This may, of course, be adapted according to the faiths represented in your school.

Prayer

Dear Lord,
Thank you God for all that you have given to us today.
Thank you for our families and our friends.
Thank you for the food we eat and the homes we live in.
Thank you the games we play, and the lessons we learn.
Thank you for helping us to remember to say thank you
for all the good things that other people do for us.
Amen

Song

Come let us remember the joys of the town (Someone's Singing Lord 7, *A&C Black*)
Thank you Lord (Come and Praise, 52: *BBC*)

Thank you

Our school community

AIM: To appreciate the school community and their place within it.

PREPARATION

■ Photocopy 'Our school community' (page 42) on to an acetate sheet ready for OHP presentation.

INTRODUCTION

Ask the children about the different groups that they belong to. If they have difficulty coming up with ideas you could start them off by saying that two groups you are part of are: your family and name a club or organisation that you belong to. Accept contributions from pupils about the groups they belong to – they may have suggestions such as school, their class within the school, groups within the class, rainbows, beavers, brownies, cubs, ballet, football, etc. Explain that you are going to introduce a word to them that they have probably heard before and that has a special meaning – the word 'community'.

ASSEMBLY

People living in one area – a village, town or city district can be seen as a community. Each local community has its own needs and these are different from place to place. A city community is very different from a countryside community. At this point you could talk about the local church or other religious communities.

Explain that a group of people who meet regularly and care about each other can also be known as a community. Discuss the school as a community. Ask pupils to suggest people that make up the school community. Answers should include children, teachers, classroom assistants, office staff, caretaker, cleaners, crossing patrol, kitchen staff, midday supervisors and, if appropriate, grounds staff. You could mention some of these people by name.

Reveal the title on the OHP and help the pupils read the word 'community'. Then read the poem to or with the pupils. Discuss the characters in the illustrations, pointing out that the people involved are all members of the school community.

REFLECTION

Encourage the children to think about the effort that needs to be put in by everybody for the school community to be a happy and successful one. Ask them to think about the importance of their role in this community and how important it is that everyone follows the rules and shows consideration for each other in their every day actions.

Prayer

Dear Lord,
Please help us to be part of the community that makes our school a happy, caring place.
Help us to think about the needs of others before ourselves and to follow the rules that keep
us safe and happy. May we try our hardest each day and do our very best in every way.
Thank you for all the people who work together to make our school community a success.
We think about the children, the teachers, the classroom assistants, the office staff, the
caretaker, the cleaners, the crossing patrol, and the kitchen staff. So many people help to
make our school a special community.

Amen

Song   Song of blessing (Everyone's Singing Lord, 37: *A&C Black*)

Our school community

I meet with all my friends
Going to school each day.
I like to learn new things
But best of all is play.

I'm helped to cross the road
The cars are stopped for me.
I'm cared for while I eat my lunch
And when I hurt my knee.

Cleaners and caretakers
Keep school clean and bright.
They work before I come to school
And when I've left at night.

With help from all the teachers
And following the rules,
The people all around me
Make this the best of schools.

The summer term

AIM: To consider summer and the changes that take place across the four months of the summer term and the summer holidays.

PREPARATION

- You may decide to delay using this assembly until early May.
- Photocopy 'The summer term' (page 44) on to an acetate sheet, for display on the OHP, but cover it with a piece of paper so that you can reveal the months one at a time.

INTRODUCTION

Explain to the children that this is now the summer term but that it isn't summer yet as it is still springtime.

ASSEMBLY

Turn on the OHP but keep the acetate covered with a piece of paper.

Does anyone know what month it is now?

Hopefully the children will say that it is the month of May. Move the paper down the screen to reveal the word *May* then discuss the fact that May is a spring month and a time when lots of changes happen very quickly – leaves grow on the trees, the grass grows and has to be cut regularly and the birds are busy making nests, laying eggs and raising their young.

What month comes after May?

Move the paper down the screen then discuss the month of *June*, when spring turns to summer and it's light until late in the evening so we can sit or play outside and enjoy the warm weather.

What month comes after June?

Move the paper down and discuss the month of *July*, which is sometimes very hot and which comes at the end of the summer term when the holidays start.

What month comes after July?

Remove the paper altogether to show all four months. Discuss the month of August when we have the school holidays and lots of people go away for their holidays.

It would be worth reminding the children of this assembly at the start of each of the following three months – learning the order of the months of the year is an objective for Year 1 pupils.

REFLECTION

Remind the children about the changes that will take place across the summer term – the leaves appearing on the trees, the weather getting warmer and sometimes getting really hot, the long evenings for playing outside.

Prayer

Dear Lord,
Thank you for the changing seasons. We thank you for the warmer weather that is starting and for the fun that we can have playing outside on the grass. Help us to enjoy the summer term. Help us to work hard at school, help us to make new friends and help us to enjoy being together, playing together and working together.

Amen

Song The flowers that grow in the garden (Someone's Singing Lord, 53: *A&C Black*)

The summer term

May

June

July

August

Here comes the sun

 AIM: For children to understand the importance of the light given by the sun each day.

PREPARATION

- Photocopy 'Here comes the sun' (page 46) and cut out the silhouettes ready for use with the OHP during the assembly.
- It would be useful to have a bright torch and a globe to show how the sun shines on the earth in the daytime.

INTRODUCTION

Begin by asking children how they know when it's time to get out of bed in the morning. There will be a variety of answers to this but someone should volunteer the fact that it is light in the mornings.

ASSEMBLY

Ask what makes it light in the morning and someone is bound to offer 'the sun' as an answer. (At this point place the silhouette of the sun in the top corner of the OHP picture and place the silhouette of the child by the bed lower down.)

Talk to the pupils about how the sun gives us light and that is why we live our active lives during the day and use the night to sleep. You may like to explain that the earth spins around every day and that during the daytime our part of the earth is facing the sun and that is why we have daylight. At night time our part of the earth is facing away from the sun and that is why we have darkness. This can be demonstrated by turning out the lights in the hall, and then shining a bright torch on to a globe. Point out to the children that the side facing the torch has lots of light but the other side of the globe is much darker.

Ask pupils what else the sun does for us. Hopefully the children will say that it gives us warmth and that it helps the flowers, grass and trees to grow (as pupils offer their responses add the appropriate silhouettes to the picture).

REFLECTION

Remind pupils that the light from the sun each day does a lot more than wake us up in the morning, it provides warmth. It enables plants to grow and some of these plants can be used for food for us and for many animals. Help pupils to understand that without the sun, the world, as we know it, could not exist.

At this point you may wish to use the words of the suggested hymn below to encourage silent reflection.

Prayer

Dear Lord,
Thank you Lord for giving us the sun each day. We are grateful for the light that wakes us each morning and the warmth shining down during the day, for the plants that grow and all the creatures that live on the earth.

Amen

Song Think of a World Without any Flowers (Someone's Singing Lord, 15: *A&C Black*)

Here comes the sun

Flowers

AIM: To appreciate the diversity of flowers that can be found around us.

PREPARATION

- Photocopy 'Flowers' (page 48) on to an acetate sheet and cut roughly round the flower outlines for display on the OHP.
- Have coloured markers available for colouring the flowers.
- If possible, take a selection of flowers into assembly with you. This will add extra interest to the assembly but is not vital to its success.

■ INTRODUCTION

Ask pupils, if appropriate, if they have any flowers in their gardens. In areas where pupils live mainly in flats ask where they see flowers – parks, shops, etc.

■ ASSEMBLY

Ask the children if they know the names of any flowers. At this point show them, if you have any, the flowers you have brought in and see if the pupils can identify any. Present the OHP flowers and ask pupils if they recognise any of them. You could ask what colours the flowers should be – pupils could come to the front and colour the flowers appropriately.

Talk about the many varieties of flowers that grow in our gardens and parks. Remind pupils that many are beautifully scented. Talk about the fact that each flower of the same variety is unique. (If you did the potatoes assembly earlier in the school year, remind them of that.)

■ REFLECTION

Invite pupils to imagine their favourite flowers and to think about how amazing it is that each of them is different. Remind the children that flowers grow on all sorts of plants. Do they know that a daffodil grows from a bulb, that a poppy grows from a tiny seed and that apple blossom grows on the apple tree which itself has grown from an apple pip?

Prayer

Dear Lord,
We thank you for the many wonderful flowers that grow, for their colours and scents.
We love to see the flowers that grow so readily in each season of the year – for the
delicate snowdrops we see in cold weather, for the cheerful daffodils we see in the spring,
and the many brightly coloured flowers that attract the butterflies and bees to our gardens
throughout the summer months. Help us to stop and look at all these flowers as we pass
them, and to think about the marvellous plants you put in our world.

Amen

Song

English country garden (Harlequin, 22: *A&C Black*)
or
The flowers that grow in the garden (Someone's Singing Lord, 53: *A&C Black*)

Flowers

Andrew Brodie: Assembly Tomorrow KS1 © A&C Black Publishers Ltd. 2008

The Billy Goats Gruff

 AIM: To help others and to learn not to be selfish.

PREPARATION

■ Photocopy 'The Billy Goats Gruff, (page 51) on to paper or card then cut out the separate pictures.

▨ INTRODUCTION

Has anybody heard the story of 'The three Billy Goats Gruff'? Here they are. (Place the three goats on the screen.)

This is little Billy Goat Gruff. This is middle-sized Billy Goat Gruff and this is big Billy Goat Gruff.

▨ STORY

The three Billy Goats Gruff had eaten so much grass in their field that there was hardly any grass left. They wanted more grass to eat and they could see a field nearby which had lots of nice, green and juicy grass growing in it. The field with the juicy grass was on the other side of the stream and to reach it all the Billy Goats Gruff had to do was to cross a bridge. (Add the bridge to the OHP.)

But there was a problem. Under the bridge lived a fierce troll and his favourite food was Billy Goats! (Place the troll under the bridge.)

The little Billy Goat Gruff was very hungry. "I'm going over the bridge to have some nice juicy grass," he said and before the others could stop him, he set off across the bridge. (Place the little Billy Goat Gruff on the bridge.)

The hungry troll heard the clip-clop sound of little Billy Goat Gruff's hooves on the bridge and jumped out in front of him. (Place the troll on the bridge.) *"What are you doing on my bridge?" he said. "This is my bridge and I'm hungry so I'm going to eat you!"*

The little Billy Goat Gruff thought quickly, because he was a clever little Billy Goat Gruff and he said, "You don't want to eat me. I'm too small. Why don't you wait for my brother? He's much bigger than me and you'll have more food to eat from him."

The hungry troll thought this was a very good idea and he let the little Billy Goat Gruff cross the bridge into the field with the juicy grass. The little Billy Goat Gruff was delighted and started eating the grass straight away. (Place the little Billy Goat Gruff on the other side of the bridge.)

The middle-sized Billy Goat Gruff saw his little brother eating the juicy grass. "I'm going over the bridge to have some nice juicy grass," he said and before the big Billy Goat Gruff could stop him, he set off across the bridge. (Place the middle-sized Billy Goat Gruff on the bridge.)

The hungry troll heard the clip-clop sound of the middle-sized Billy Goat Gruff's hooves on the bridge and jumped out in front of him. (Place the troll on the bridge.) *"What are you doing on my bridge?" he said. "This is my bridge and I'm hungry so I'm going to eat you!"*

The middle-sized Billy Goat Gruff thought quickly and he said: "You don't want to eat me. I'm only middle-sized. Why don't you wait for my brother? He's much bigger than me and you'll have more food to eat from him."

The hungry troll thought this was a very good idea and he let the middle-sized Billy Goat Gruff cross the bridge into the field with the juicy grass. The middle-sized Billy Goat Gruff was delighted and started eating the grass straight away. (Place the middle-sized Billy Goat Gruff on the other side of the bridge.)

The Billy Goats Gruff

The big Billy Goat Gruff saw his two brothers eating the lovely juicy grass and he decided that he would cross the bridge too. "My brothers are very brave," *he said to himself,* "I will cross the bridge too." (Place the big Billy Goat Gruff on the bridge.)

The hungry troll heard the clip-clop sound of the big Billy Goat Gruff's hooves on the bridge and jumped out in front of the big Billy Goat Gruff. (Place the troll on the bridge.) "What are you doing on my bridge?" *he said.* "This is my bridge and I'm hungry so I'm going to eat you!"

"Oh, no you're not!" *said the big Billy Goat Gruff, and he pushed the troll into the stream. Then he trotted over the bridge and joined his two brothers eating the lovely, green, juicy grass.* (Place the big Billy Goat Gruff on the other side of the bridge.)

▓ REFLECTION

Ask the pupils to think about the story carefully, considering questions such as: 'Did the story have a happy ending?' 'Who behaved well in the story?' 'Who behaved badly in the story?' 'Was there a bully in the story?' Accept and discuss all the answers from the children. Ask specifically about the behaviour of the little Billy Goat Gruff and the middle-sized Billy Goat Gruff, trying to draw out the fact that they behaved selfishly, not worrying about the fate of the big Billy Goat Gruff.

Can the children relate the story to their own lives in the school community? Are they always unselfish?

Prayer

Dear Lord,
Please help us to be unselfish. Help us to help others and not to treat them unkindly.
Help us to stop bullying and the bullying of other people.

Amen

🎵

Song

Travel on, travel on (Come and Praise, 42: *BBC*)

Andrew Brodie: Assembly Tomorrow KS1 © A&C Black Publishers Ltd. 2008

Working animals

 AIM: To encourage a knowledge and appreciation of the animals that help people each day.

PREPARATION

■ Photocopy 'Working animals' (page 53) and cut out the silhouettes.
■ Have coloured markers available in case they are needed. You may decide to label pictures as you display them or add the names of animals for which there is no picture.

INTRODUCTION

Ask pupils if they know what a country show is. Has anyone been to a country show?

STORY

Billy and his parents were having a day out at a country show. Billy wasn't sure what a country show was as he had never been to one before. His mother explained to him that it would be an outdoor event and there would be all sorts of things to see and do.

On the way there, looking out of the car window, Billy noticed a young woman with a golden Labrador who was wearing a special reflective harness. The woman and her dog were going into the supermarket.

"Dogs can't usually go into shops," explained Mum, *"but that is a rather special dog known as a 'guide dog', which helps people who are unable to see."* (Place silhouette of guide dog on OHP.) *Billy was intrigued as he thought that all dogs were pets and didn't know that they could be trained to do important things like guiding people safely each day.*

They soon arrived at the show and bought a programme. To Billy's surprise he saw an item in the programme that said 'Working Dogs Display'.

"Can we watch that?" he asked excitedly. *"There will be lots of guide dogs there."*
"I really don't think it will be guide dogs," laughed his father. *"Let's go and see".*

Billy and his parents went to see the 'Working Dogs Display' but to Billy's surprise there were collie dogs that had been cleverly trained to help farmers to move sheep. (Place silhouette of collie on OHP.)

Later that day, after seeing horses, cows, pigs, sheep, visiting stalls, going on rides and listening to a brass band playing, Billy and his parent began the long drive home. As Billy sat in the car his mind drifted back to thinking about dogs and other animals that can help people. He asked his parents how else animals help us. Unfortunately he was fast asleep before they had even begun to answer him. Perhaps you can think of some that you know about.

Ask pupils if they know any animals that are specially trained to help people. Accept their answers and where applicable add silhouettes to the OHP. Where a sensible answer is offered but the picture is not available write the idea on the OHP sheet. Responses will vary but may include sniffer dogs, dogs that are trained to help the disabled, German Shepherds to help police to search and detain, St. Bernards trained for search and rescue and Newfoundland, trained for rescue in the water.

REFLECTION

Ask the children to think about the huge difference a working animal can make to the life of a person – the best way to do this is to pick one type of animal and consider the differences made by that one animal. A good example would be a guide dog or 'seeing dog for the blind'. The children may remember the assembly 'Look into my eyes' on page 27.

Prayer

Dear Lord,
We thank you for all the animals that help people each day, for those that can help to keep people safe and those who can help us to move heavy loads or even rescue us from danger. Please bless all the wonderful creatures that help us. Amen

Song

All things, which live below the sky (Someone's Singing Lord, 41: *A&C Black*)

A happy playground

AIM: To encourage consideration and co-operation between pupils, especially at playtime.

PREPARATION

■ Photocopy 'A happy playground' (page 55) and cut out the silhouettes for use on the OHP during this assembly.

■ INTRODUCTION

Ask pupils to show (perhaps by raising their hands) which of them enjoy school playtimes. (It will be interesting to note as this point if any pupils do not raise their hands – perhaps the assembly will be of more relevance to these children.)

■ ASSEMBLY

Ask the children to think about and then tell you about the different things they like to do at playtime. Accept their contributions and where an answer has a matching silhouette place this on the overhead projector.

Explain that you are pleased that so many of them like to play these games. Then tell them that there is one more picture of a child at playtime that they have not yet seen. (Add the 'sad' silhouette to the scene, but do not use any term that suggests that this figure is unhappy. Ensure that it is placed a little distance from the happier ones.)

Ask the children what they think the new picture represents. Accept their answers and ask them why they think this person is not playing happily. You are likely to get answers that infer the child is lonely or has no one to play with. Finally ask pupils to think about any occasion when they might have felt lonely in the playground. You may wish to have a show of hands for this.

■ REFLECTION

Ask pupils if there is any way that they can make sure that there are never lonely children in their playground. They will readily suggest that they can ask the lonely child to join in their games.

Discuss the fact that, even if the lonely child is not one of their special friends, they can make the playground a caring place by including him/her in their play.

Prayer

Dear Lord,
Help us to make our playground a caring place, and to remember to consider the happiness of others each and every day. Help to make us the sort of children that are generous enough to share smiles, games and cheerfulness with each other.

Amen

Song

Jesus' hands were kind hands (Someone's Singing Lord, 33: *A&C Black*)

Andrew Brodie: Assembly Tomorrow KS1 © A&C Black Publishers Ltd. 2008

A happy playground

Through the window

AIM: To compare possible views through a window, appreciating nature and making judgments about less attractive features.

PREPARATION

■ Photocopy 'Through the window' (page 57) on to an acetate sheet and place it on the OHP.

■ Photocopy the silhouette of the window-frame (page 58) and place it on top of the acetate sheet so that the four pictures will show through the window panes but cover each pane with a separate piece of paper. You could also draw some extra pictures on a separate acetate sheet to show things that could potentially be seen through a window.

INTRODUCTION

If possible, in your school hall, ask the pupils to look out of the window and to describe what they can see. Encourage them to look carefully, prompting them to notice as much as possible. If this is not possible in your setting, ask the children to close their eyes and to try to remember what they can see out of a window in their house. You will not be able to accept everyone's answers but ask a few children what they can see through their window at home.

ASSEMBLY

Turn on the OHP to show the window.

Look at this window – what can we see through this window?

(Remove the first piece of paper to reveal the picture at the top left.) Discuss the bird and how it's good to see birds flying in the sky.

(Remove the paper to reveal the picture at the bottom left.) Stress the fact that it's an attractive flower. (Now remove the paper from the top right to reveal the smoke.)

That's not such a good view is it? All that smoke is not good for us – and what about the view through this part of the window?

(Reveal the final picture in the bottom right.)

What do we see?

Encourage the children to identify the litter.

Litter is not good because it makes the world untidy and it can be very dangerous for wild animals such as hedgehogs.

REFLECTION

Encourage the pupils to consider good things that we can see through the window and the not so good things.

Is there any way that we can improve the view from our window? What can all of us do to try to stop views becoming spoilt?

Help the pupils to realise that we all have an impact on the environment and that we have a responsibility not to drop litter or cause pollution.

Prayer

♪

Song

Dear Lord,
Help us all to protect our environment by not dropping litter and spoiling our streets and our countryside. We thank you for the lovely flowers, birds and animals. Help us all to protect them. Amen

This is a lovely world (Someone's Singing Lord, 8: *A&C Black*)

Andrew Brodie: Assembly Tomorrow KS1 © A&C Black Publishers Ltd. 2008

Through the window

Through the window 2

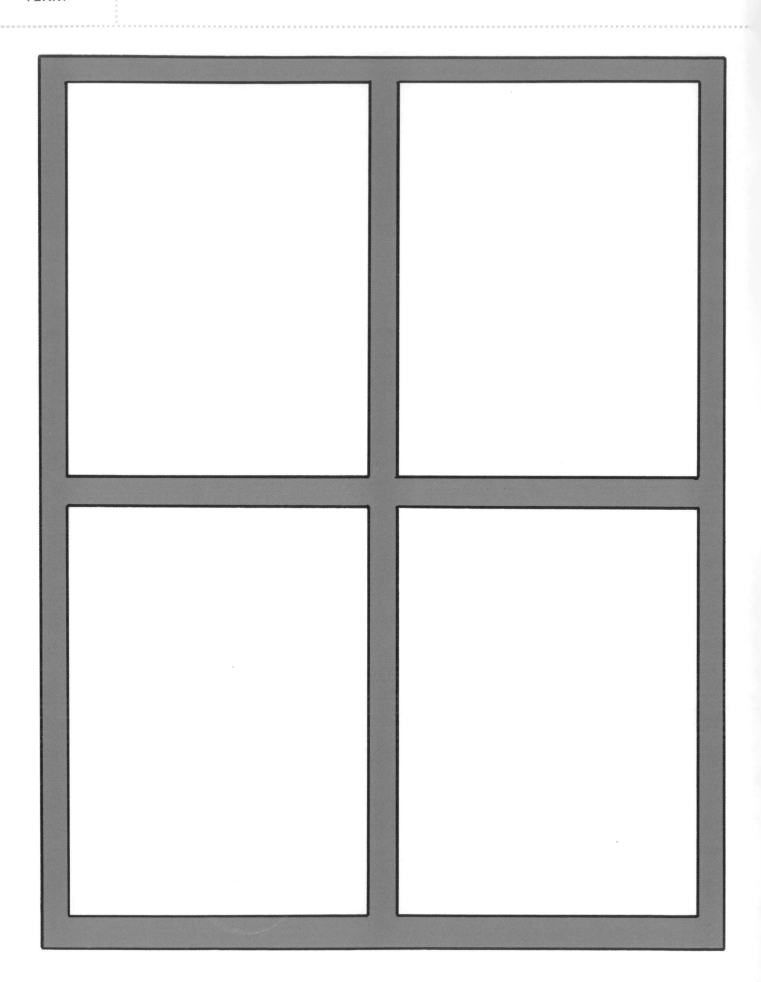

Clever Crow

 AIM: To think about why we should ignore bullies and focus on our achievements.

PREPARATION

■ Photocopy 'Clever Crow' (page 60) on to an acetate sheet for display on the OHP.

■ You could cut out some pieces of paper to place over the picture of the jug to represent the rising water level. Alternatively, you could use a real glass jug with water in and demonstrate the process described in the story.

INTRODUCTION

This story has been adapted from one of Aesop's fables. Ask the children not to name anyone in particular but to describe what a bully does. Help them to understand that a bully is someone who makes fun of other people and sometimes even hurts them.

ASSEMBLY

Turn on the OHP to show the picture of the crows and pebbles, but cover the picture of the jug until the appropriate point in the story.

This is the story of Clever Crow. He was very clever but he was also very sad because some of the other crows used to bully him. They would call him names and make fun of him although he never did anything mean to them.

One very hot day the crows were very thirsty. It hadn't rained for weeks and the ponds had all dried up. All the crows were desperate for a drink, which made them very bad-tempered and even meaner to Clever Crow.

Clever Crow took no notice of the bullies. He tried not to care. What he did care about though was how thirsty he was. Then he spotted a big glass jug, which had some water in it. He flew down to the jug and tried to get a drink but he couldn't get his head far enough down inside the jug to reach the water.

In desperation he looked around and on the ground he spotted some pebbles. He had a great idea because he was a very clever crow. He picked up one of the pebbles and dropped it carefully into the water. Then he picked up another and another and another. He kept picking up pebbles and dropping them into the jug and as he did so the level of the water got higher and higher. Soon the water was high enough for Clever Crow to have a drink. He gulped the water down and felt so much better.

The other crows saw him drinking and flew over to have a drink themselves.

REFLECTION

Encourage the children to think about the story and the morals it contains and, in particular, to discuss this final question.

Do you think Clever Crow should have shared his water with the others?

Prayer

Dear Lord,
Please give us the strength to deal with bullies, to not be frightened of bullies and to get on with our lives whatever bullies may say or do to us. Please help us to never bully anyone else. Help us always to be kind to each other.

Amen

Song   Look out for loneliness (Someone's Singing Lord, 36: *A&C Black*)

Andrew Brodie: Assembly Tomorrow KS1 © A&C Black Publishers Ltd. 2008

Clever Crow

Clever Chris

AIM: To think about why we should ignore bullies and focus on our own achievements.

PREPARATION

■ Photocopy 'Clever Chris' (page 62) and cut out the silhouettes of the boy and the ball .

▥ INTRODUCTION

Remind the children of the story of 'Clever Crow'. Ask them not to name anyone in particular but to describe what a bully does. Help them understand that a bully is someone who makes fun of other people and sometimes even hurts other people.

▥ ASSEMBLY

Turn on the OHP to show the silhouette of Clever Chris.

This is the story of Clever Chris. He was a very clever boy but he was also very sad because some of the other children used to bully him. They would call him names and make fun of him although he never did anything mean to them.

One of the things that the bullies did to Clever Chris was to make fun of him when he was doing PE, especially when it involved throwing or catching a ball. The problem was that although Clever Chris was good at most things he couldn't seem to throw or catch a ball properly. When he threw it, it went the wrong way and when he tried to catch it, it slipped through his fingers. The bullies thought this was very funny and they laughed at him and sometimes other children in the class would laugh at him too.

Clever Chris was clever and so he decided he would try to do something about the problem. Without telling anybody, he started practising at home. Every day he would go outside with a ball and throw it against the wall. He picked a spot on the wall to aim for and he threw the ball quite gently at that spot. Usually he missed and the ball would roll away and he would have to go and fetch it but he practised and practised until slowly he began to get better. His catching improved too.

In the PE lesson at school one day the teacher announced that it was time to do some throwing and catching practice. Everyone had to fetch a ball from the basket and just throw the ball in the air and catch it again. The bullies began to snigger when they thought about Clever Chris and what a mess he would make of it.

"Start now," said the teacher. Everyone started throwing the ball up and catching it when it came down. The bullies were quite good at it but Clever Chris was the best. He threw and he caught, he threw and he caught, over and over again. Everybody was amazed and even the bullies couldn't laugh at Clever Chris any more.

▥ REFLECTION

Encourage the children to think about the story and the morals it contains and, in particular, to discuss this final question: *How did Clever Chris manage to get better at throwing and catching?*

Prayer

Dear Lord,
Please give us the strength to deal with bullies, to not be frightened of bullies and to get on with our lives whatever bullies may say or do to us. Please help us never to bully anyone else. Help us always to be kind to each other. Help us to have the strength to keep practising things that we find difficult – it's not easy to get better but help us to keep trying.
Amen

Song   Look out for loneliness (Someone's Singing Lord, 36: *A&C Black*)

Clever Chris

Holidays

 AIM: To appreciate the variety of experiences that can enrich our lives.

PREPARATION

- Photocopy 'Holidays' (page 64) and have it ready for OHP presentation. The poem 'At the seaside' is by Robert Louis Stevenson.
- If possible have a holiday souvenir, postcard or other holiday item, e.g. plane ticket or bucket and spade. If you do not have a suitable item then miss out the first item in the introduction below.

INTRODUCTION

Firstly, show the children your visual aid and ask them what it makes them think of. Accept answers that refer to 'holidays'. Explain that, as it is now nearly the summer holidays, today's assembly is all about holidays. You may like to ask the children what they will be doing during the long summer break from school. Some children will be going away on holiday but there are many who will not. These children can be reminded that they will still have a good break from school so that they can come back to school in the autumn term refreshed and ready to enjoy school work again! Encourage them to think of all the good things they will be doing, such as playing in the garden, going to the shops with parents or grandparents, riding their bikes, going to the park, etc.

ASSEMBLY

Show pupils the OHP picture and ask them about each element. Ask how pupils might have travelled to their holiday destinations. Match their responses to the pictures around the poem. Read the poem with them and discuss the enjoyment of playing on the beach. Ask pupils whether they have been to the seaside for a holiday. Discuss the type of things they might do on the beach – paddling in the sea, digging holes in the sand, building sandcastles, having picnics, etc. You may like to take the opportunity of reminding children of safety when playing on beaches such as staying near their parents, not going in the water alone, etc. Ask what other sorts of holidays there are. Some children will be lucky enough to have a wide experience of holidays, including skiing, canal boats, pony trekking, etc. Others will have more limited experiences and some sensitivity may be required to ensure that they are not made to feel less important. Accept all appropriate responses including that of having day trips during the school holidays.

REFLECTION

Encourage pupils to think about how they feel when they are looking forward to a holiday and when they are actually on holiday. Explain that some people never get a holiday throughout their whole lives. Many people throughout the world never travel further than it is possible to go on foot.

Prayer

Dear Lord,
We thank you for the holidays that we have – for the days out, the travel to new places in your wonderful world and for seeing new things. Bless all those who make the enjoyment of our holidays possible.

Amen

Song   This beautiful world (Everyone's singing Lord, 2: *A&C Black*)

Holidays

At the seaside

By Robert Louis Stevenson

When I was down beside the sea
A wooden spade they gave to me
To dig the sandy shore.
My holes were like an empty cup,
In every hole the sea came up
Till it could come no more.